The Place Of Tales
A Kid's Guide To Canterbury, Kent, England

Photography By John D. Weigand
Poetry By Penelope Dyan

Bellissima Publishing, LLC
Jamul, California
www.bellissimapublishing.com

copyright © 2011 by Penny D. Weigand

All rights reserved. No part of this book may be
reproduced or transmitted in any form or by any means,
electronic or mechanical, including photocopying,
recording, or by any other means, or by any information or
storage retrieval system, without permission from the publisher.

ISBN 978-1-935630-66-1
First Edition

*For Pilgrims who Travel Afar
And To Mr. Debrout,
Wherever You Are!*

The Place Of Tales
Bellissima Publishing, LLC

Introduction

The Canterbury Tales begin with the introduction of a group of pilgrims journeying to Canterbury to the shrine of Thomas Becket. The pilgrims include a knight, his son (the Squire) the knight's yeoman, a prioress (a kind of nun), a second nun, a monk, a friar, a merchant, a clerk, a man of law, a franklin, a weaver, a dyer, a carpenter, a tapestry-maker, a haberdasher, a cook, a shipman, a physician, a parson, a miller, a manciple, a reeve, a summoner, a pardoner, the wife of Bath, and the author of the Canterbury tales, himself, Geoffrey Chaucer! They meet at the Tabard Inn and decide to tell stories to pass the time on the way to Canterbury. The host of the Tabard Inn sets the rules for the tales. Each pilgrim is to tell two stories on the way to Canterbury, and two stories on their return. The host will decide whose tale is best for meaningfulness and for fun. They draw lots to decide who will tell the first tale, and the knight wins. The trip and the tales follow, and the interesting thing is that many of the sayings we use so often today come straight from "The Canterbury Tales" and Geoffrey Chaucer.

Penelope Dyan and John D. Weigand traveled to Canterbury, UK so that you could see the destination of these pilgrims. Now while the original tales are told in old English, there is now a version of them everyone can easily understand. The importance of these tales and knowing all about them is that this is the foundation that actually began English literature, and if you know about Chaucer. you will be ahead in your future studies. It is also important to know these tales as a stepping stone for telling and writing stories of your own, because the creation of stories is what Dyan, an award winning writer, former teacher and attorney, wants you to do! Every kid should use his or her imagination to its fullest! Everyone has a story to tell, and this is the whole point of Chaucer's Canterbury tales as well!

The Place Of Tales
Bellissima Publishing, LLC

The Place of Tales
A Kid's Guide To Canterbury, Kent, England

Photography By John D. Weigand
Poetry By Penelope Dyan

If it's a pilgrimage to Canterbury that you make,
when you get to Canterbury you'll see the gate.*

* Westgate is the largest surviving city gate in England. The entrance was originally protected by wooden doors, a portcullis and a draw-bridge.

As you pass through the gate and walk down the shadowy street,
other pilgrims, town's folk, and shop owners you'll happily greet!

And if about William Chaucer and his Canterbury tales you want to learn more, you might want to step into this used book store!
And don't you think it would be grand to walk out with a copy of Chaucer's Canterbury Tales in your hand?

In this store you can get some Cornish pasties to eat. . .

Or you can go to a bakery and buy cookies (made for kids) especially sweet.

The shops and stores are very quaint,
some colored brightly in black and white paint!
You can find absolutely everything there,
even brand new underwear!

You can travel down the River Stour,
(Check with the tour guide for time and hour.)
At the very beginning of the river
you can just get on a boat,
And past beautiful Canterbury
you can float.
And you will hear stories of history,
and you will see lots of stuff,
Of which you can NEVER learn quite enough!
Because when all is said and done,
this kind of learning is LOTS of fun!

This building sells pizza right here,
But it didn't ALWAYS sell such food, my dear.
It was once a medieval forge,
and not a place to just eat and gorge!

This was once used as the potty bridge,
And if the potty board broke-----
you fell into WATER, as COLD as a FRIDGE!

You'll see a church of stone with flowers bright,
You'll wonder if it hosted a famous knight.
You'll wonder if the knights of Chaucer's day--
traveled past HERE as THEY went on their way.

Under buildings of brick you will gently float,
along with the others in your small boat.
Pilgrims of all sorts you are, all traveling here
(like Chaucer's pilgrims) from afar.
But I wonder, did you EACH tell a story
FILLED with images of courage and glory?

As you float past the old weavers house,
you'll stare from the boat like a quiet mouse.
Here they have a ducking stool.
You were dunked in water for just being a fool.
And when a husband became really gruff,
he would dunk his wife when he'd had enough.
This is true, and to this I swear.
It was humiliating (for her) and QUIET unfair!

And this 1237 building, so very old,
Is the Dominican Priory, or so I am told!
And you'll wonder why it was, that they all went,
to the River Stour in Canturbury, Kent!

And as your boat goes around the bend,
You realize your journey is about to end.

You get out of the boat
and you walk back down the street,
with years of history beneath your feet.
You imagine EVERYTHING you heard
about Chaucer; IT'S true!
And NOW it is quite clear to you.
The magic of Canterbury is all around,
You know other wonderful tales of Canterbury
must abound.
So like Chaucer's pilgrims and Chaucer's knight,
you think of your own tale to tell,
and you just sit down and WRITE!

Quotes From The Father Of English Literature

"And she was fair as is the rose in May."
"By nature, men love newfangledness. "
"Filth and old age, I'm sure you will agree, are powerful wardens upon chastity."
"First he wrought, and afterward he taught."
"Forbid us something, and that thing we desire. "
"Love is blind."
"Nowhere so busy a man as he than he, and yet he seemed busier than he was."
"The guilty think all talk is of themselves."
"The life so short, the crafts so long to learn."
"There's never a new fashion but it's old."
"There's no workman, whatsoever he be, That may both work well and hastily."
"Time and tide wait for no man."
"She loved right from the first sight."
"It is not all gold that glareth."

Geoffrey Chaucer
c. 1343 – 25 October 1400

Geoffrey Chaucer is known as the Father of English literature, is considered to be the greatest English poet of the Middle Ages.

www.ingramcontent.com/pod-product-compliance
Ingram Content Group UK Ltd.
Pitfield, Milton Keynes, MK11 3LW, UK
UKHW060137240426
12048UKWH00002B/72